Words from the Chief

A selection of MacArthur and Scottish History articles by
James Edward Moir MacArthur of that Ilk, FSA Scot
Late Chief of Clan Arthur

Edited by Hugh DP McArthur, FSA Scot
Illustrated by Roy Boyd

Published by House of Arthur
© clannarthur.com 2006
ISBN: 0-9551920-0-5

PRINTED IN SCOTLAND

Contents

Foreword

By Hugh DP McArthur

From beyond the veils of ancient times, Clan Arthur has been a powerful influence in shaping Britain and the world we know today. Claiming descent from the legendary King Arthur and lending their support to the later legends of Wallace and Bruce, MacArthur earned his respected place in early Highland society. In 1427, the power and bond of the great Argyll family was broken with the beheading of their leader, John MacArthur. Since that time Clan Arthur's story has been all but eclipsed by the rise of the younger brother Campbell Clan.

Clan Arthur's chiefly line continued after 1427, albeit with much reduced status, till the last chief, Patrick MacArthur, died in Jamaica in 1771. Since that day the Chiefship of Clan Arthur has lain vacant and the history of Arthur's Children has been lost.

In 1991, Robert McArthur in Scotland, organised a *derbfine* (a meeting of the arms bearing members of the clan) and a number of suitably qualified clansmen duly made their way home to Argyll to hold council. At the *derbfine's* request James Edward Moir MacArthur of the Ancient and Noble House of Milton was proposed to the Lord Lyon King of Arms as the new leader of Clan Arthur. In 1992 the *derbfine's* petition was upheld, and James MacArthur was appointed Commander of Clan Arthur with a primary task of tracing Clan Arthur's true chief.

After eleven years' further genealogical research, James Edward Moir MacArthur of the Ancient and Noble Houses of Tirivadich and Milton lodged a petition with the Lord Lyon. The Lord Lyon again upheld this petition and on 28 August 2002, James Edward Moir MacArthur of that Ilk was appointed the first Chief of Clan Arthur after an absence of 231 years. On 13 April 2003, near a hundred MacArthur kin met in Edinburgh, and James Edward Moir MacArthur of that Ilk was accepted and duly inaugurated Chief of

FOREWORD

Clan Arthur.

This booklet is a collection of articles written by the Chief. These words reflect his rare and intimate knowledge gathered through a lifetime of passion for his clan, culture and country. Clan Arthur's battle cry is *Eisd O' Eisd* (Listen O' Listen). Now listen to the *Words from the Chief.*

In Search of the Motto

FIDE ET OPERA

Back in 1948, the then Lord Lyon King of
Arms, Sir Thomas Innes of Learney,
K.C.V.O., Advocate, wrote on page 59 of
the 4th edition of his excellent book
The Tartans and Families of Scotland, as follows:

> *To prevent mistakes in battle, and fraud in sealing deeds,
> etc., the King had to arrange for control of heraldry and settlement
> of disputes. Since this involved genealogy the matter was delegated
> to the Royal Seannachie of Celtic Scotland, as chief genealogist,
> who became the Lord Lyon King of Arms, and who—since he repre-
> sents the King—was given a tabard of the Royal Arms. It was soon
> held that only arms granted or confirmed by Lyon was admissible.
> In 1592 and 1672, the Scottish Parliament forbade the use of arms
> not so confirmed, and established the 'Public Register of all Arms
> and Bearings in Scotland', which is kept in the Court of the Lord
> Lyon, H.M. Register House, Edinburgh. Under the Act of Parliament
> it is unlawful to use any arms which have not been matriculated in
> that Register, or to use the registered arms of any person of whom
> you are not the lawful heir; i.e., senior living descendant in terms of
> patent or last confirmation.*

Each Scottish coat of arms is granted to one person by name
only, and not to a family. In 1672 the Public Register was started and
continues to this day.

Let us now see if where the motto 'Fide et Opera' came from
can be found. The first recorded MacArthur coat of arms was granted
by the Lord Lyon to Archibald MacArthur Stewart (1749-1815) of
Milton and Ascog on 5th April 1775. A copy of the original documentation is to be found at folio 506 of volume 1 of *Scottish Coats of*

Arms in the Lord Lyon's office. Milton is at Dunoon in Cowal, Argyll, and Ascog is on the Isle of Bute, near Rothesay. As volume 1 was presumably started in 1672, it would appear that it had taken over 100 years to grant and record about 500 coats of arms, unless more than one storage volume was in use. It is quite different today, where the Lyon office is a very busy place.

Now, once a coat of arms has been granted, a Herald Painter prepares two written and hand-painted copies of the description and achievement on vellum. One of these is kept in the large folio-sized covers in the office of the Lyon Court, and the other, once the paint and handwritten authority has dried, is sent specially packed to the successful petitioner. At the end of 1995 there were 78 such volumes, and that number will have materially increased by now, due to the interest in Scottish coats of arms, not only by individual persons but by commercial businesses as well, for they also can be granted and use arms.

Lost records

The name of the Lord Lyon in 1775 was John Hooke-Campbell, he holding that important post from 1754 to 1796. The 9th Earl of Kinnoull, Robert Auriol Hay, then became Lord Lyon till 1804. At that time there was no recognized Lyon Court office for the Lord Lyon or his Lyon Clerk, that came later, and as there was comparatively little storage required for official papers and documents and volumes of coats of arms, some were kept by the Lord Lyon and the rest by his Lyon Clerk in their own homes. The 9th Earl of Kinnoull owned and often lived at Dupplin Castle, some 6 miles southwest of Perth, and in about 1798 when the Earl was in residence there was a fire and the Lyon Court records which were with him were destroyed.

This could possibly explain why there is no documentation pertaining to a MacArthur coat of arms with motto prior to 1775. It is, however, shown in the list of successful students that Archibald's father, John MacArthur (c.1708-1772) of Milton was armigerous in

1766, when Glasgow University awarded his son, student 2579, his law degree, later becoming an advocate. Further, in volume 7, page 65, published in 1992 by the Royal Commission on the Ancient and Historical Monuments of Scotland for mid Argyll and Cowal, there is printed within column 1 the following, regarding a flat gravestone on six supports adjacent to the front door in the churchyard of the High Kirk of Dunoon. The church was originally dedicated in 1270 and rebuilt in 1816, being worshipped in every Sunday still.

Funerary Monuments. The following monuments are in the churchyard, which also contains several other 18th century monuments.

(1) Table-tomb with moulded edges and elaborate legs, very worn. It bears emblems of mortality in relief, then a shield which is completely defaced. A marginal inscription reads:

> **(HER)E LIES JOHN M(AC) A(R)THU(R O)F**
> **MILNTOUN WHO DECEASED THE 1[?]**
> **OF A(V)G(VST) 1674 AND OF HIS A(GE) [?5] 0**

A secondary inscription commemorates John MacArthur of Milton and his wife, Mary Sandilands, with the date 1772. The first-named John MacArthur founded a family which held a considerable estate in the Dunoon area until the 19th century.

As there was originally a shield cut into this raised gravestone, it might just be that John's (c.1708-1772) great grandfather, John MacArthur (c.1615-1674) of Milntoun had a coat of arms, or at least some type of crest (with motto?), which has now completely weathered away on the shield on the flat gravestone.

Nomenclature of a Coat of Arms

The full achievement of a basic Scottish coat of arms—and no two may be the same—consists of, from the base, a shield on which the actual arms are shown, a helmet, mantling suspended from the helmet, a wreath, a crest, and a motto. In granting a new coat of arms the whole of the achievement is discussed by the Lord Lyon with the petitioner, and once agreed and granted the motto remains with that achievement, though over time there may be differences on the shield. The eldest son takes his father's coat of arms on his father's death, and should notify the Lord Lyon of the occurrence.

In olden times very few people could write, and so each member of the nobility down even to the smaller landowner was obliged to have his own seal in order to sign land transactions and other official documents. Seal engravers had a good trade, especially the better known ones. They cut the seal in reverse onto steel, which would then be fitted to a suitable holder, but in the case of signet rings straight into the gold. The resulting seal in wax on parchment or paper would correctly produce a positive image in relief. Seals, if large enough, could show the shield from a coat of arms or, more often if smaller, just the crest of those entitled persons. For those not holding such insignia it was the duty of the sealmaker to produce something suitable, without impinging on heraldic law. This was not always the case.

Tirivadich Chief

The head of the family of Tirivadich, on Lochaweside, was shown by documentary proof to have been the Chief of the Clan Arthur in 1569. However, no coat of arms is presently traceable. So, all that can be said is that, if he did possess a coat of arms—and there is no proof that he did—then the shield might have been on a blue ground, three antique gold crowns each with five spikes, possibly surrounding a silver coloured cross Moline. The motto of 'Fide et Opera' (By Faith and Work) in Latin, in which language most mottoes were written in former times, was only first recorded in 1775, when Archibald MacArthur Stewart of Milton and Ascog was granted his coat of arms, as mentioned above. Leaving aside the Stewart of Ascog (which property was inherited by him in 1771), being part of Archibald's combined coat of arms, his shield for MacArthur of Milton only showed three antique gold crowns, each with five spikes, on a blue ground, surrounding a Maltese cross in a silver colour.

Before we examine the motto, let us look at these three golden crowns. Where did they come from back in 1775 or earlier? Some researchers say that they originally represented someone Scottish in the Middle Ages with leadership qualities, and could possibly be connected with the areas of Cumbria, Northumbria and Strathclyde, which in former times stretched from northern Argyll to south of Carlisle in England. But then others maintain that the three areas were Northumbria in England together with the three Lothians and the whole of central Scotland as far west as Dumbarton Castle. Be that as it may, let us now look at page 8 of volume 2 of *A System of Heraldry* by Alexander Nisbet, published in Edinburgh in 1816.

King Henry V (of England) died in France on the last day of August 1422. His body was brought to Rouen, in order to be conveyed to England, and put in a lead coffin, and placed in a chariot drawn by four horses. Upon the covering of the four horses that drew the chariot were embroidered the arms of England alone; upon the second horse the arms of France and England quarterly; upon the cover of the third horse the arms of France alone; and on the fourth the arms of King Arthur, viz. azure three crowns in pale or.

"Azure" equals the colour blue. "In pale" means down the center of the shield. "Or" indicates a golden colour.

Connection to Arms of King Arthur?

Could the three crowns for King Arthur (who is said to have lived c.475-542 in southwest England, with jurisdiction over Brittany and a large section of Wales) be part of the ancient clan shield in the present-day MacArthur coats of arms, or do they come from one of the areas in Scotland mentioned above? Or, is there some other quite different explanation, such as an early connection to the Lennox area of Scotland? Let us not get involved in that meantime, but having prepared the ground we can now look at the subject of this lengthy treatise.

Fide et Opera

In Latin, 'fides' means faith, trust, honour or loyalty: while 'opus' is work or workmanship. The word 'fides' becomes 'fide' when in the ablative singular (that is, when placing 'by,' 'with,' or 'from' before the noun). The word 'opus' becomes 'opera' when in the nominative plural; i.e., 'works.' Occasionally there has been confusion in the translating of the motto into English, but it should strictly read 'By Faith and Works'. However, through time the second noun has come to be use collectively, so for 'works' read 'work'; that is to say 'By Faith and Work' is our motto today.

Motto translations vary

Very unfortunately, other translations can be found in several good Scottish publications, such as 'By Fidelity and Labour'. But from where did this exhortation come? To find it, please turn to the New Testament in the Bible. Look for the Book of James, chapter 2, and start reading at verse 14. When you have read to verse 28 you will have found the MacArthur motto has been fully explained. It also shows why so many MacArthurs over the years have accomplished so many good and memorable things for the sake of their families as well as for all mankind. From ancient times, it is true, that we have not always been popular, being by nature somewhat strong willed and at times irascible, but on the whole we all—man, woman, or child— consciously or unconsciously try to live by our most worthwhile motto, no matter from where it originated in Scotland.

 The following could be of interest to those who make a study of times past. My grandfather James (1843-1917) of Milton, Dunoon, Argyll, and of Hillfoot, Dollar, which is in Clackmannanshire, was a conscientious elder of the kirk. Each morning in his home he held a short service for all the family and indoor staff, and he would read a chapter from the Bible. He did not make use of the Family Bible (10 by 8 inches), printed in 1755 by Thomas Baskett the printer to the University of Oxford, because it was too large and heavy to conveniently handle. The handwritten family records in that Bible start with the year 1709. It has recently been rebound. Instead, James used a smaller Bible (7 by 5 inches), published in 1863 by William Collins, Licensed Queen's Printer, in Glasgow. Each day after reading from a chapter James would comment on the passage, and would make a note in pencil in the margin of the page in the Bible of the date, thus avoiding repetition. Accordingly, it is gratifying to find, on looking at the New Testament in the Glasgow Bible, that James, chapter 2, verses 14 to 28, was read and re-marked on Friday, 28th November, 1898. I never met my paternal Grandfather, but I am led to believe he lived up to our motto.

While it has not been possible to establish, as yet, how long ago the MacArthur motto came to be first used and recognized, other than the date of 1775, it should not be forgotten that there are two ancient Gaelic sayings, which both refer to the considerable age of our worldwide family.

"The hills and streams and MacAlpin
But from whence came forth MacArthur?"

"There is none older, save the hills
The Devil and MacArthur."

The Clan Arthur Tartan

Some weeks ago I received an enquiry about the Tartan of the Clan MacArthur, and as a result I did some research to fill out the knowledge which I already had on the subject. I know about our present tartan, but I had found out early in 1988 that there had been another MacArthur Tartan, which was more than likely older than the one presently used. So there are two Clan MacArthur Tartans, not dissimilar. Let us now go back in time.

It would appear that the beginning of Highland dress started with the links that Scotland had with Ireland, and the emigration of Gaelic speaking Irishmen to Argyllshire and to the adjacent Inner Islands of the Hebrides, in the 7th century. The early Scots wore a longish saffron or other brightly coloured shirt plus a mantle. They also sometimes, according to their status wore trews, which were tight fitting, and resembled footed leggings, reaching from the waist down each leg separately to the ankle. This garment was known in Gaelic as *tribubhas*. The Book of the Kells in the 9th century refers to them. About 1095 AD a Norwegian King returned home from a visit to the Hebrides adopted the costume worn there, and he went about barelegged, wearing only a short tunic and an upper garment, which must have left a lot of the body without covering. An early form of sporran, in which to carry provisions, was first mentioned, as far as can be found, about 1105. Roughly one hundred years later the first actual evidence of Highland dress was found in carved walrus ivory chessmen, which show military Highlanders. These were discovered at Uig in the Isle of Lewis. Three centuries on, that is to say about 1400, stone effigies on Islay and in western Ireland show it could have been a long sleeved coat with vertical quilting. Early in the 16th century the Highlander for everyday use still wore no clothing from the middle of his thigh shirt to his feet, but covered himself with a saffron coloured shirt and a mantel. However, some Clan Chiefs had begun to have special weave made for them individually, which in time could or would have developed in to the Clan Tartan. It must be noted that the word 'tartan' does not exist in the Gaelic language, and is most likely derived from the French word *tiretaine* or the Spanish word *tiritana*, simply meaning a coloured woollen material, which of course the cloth in the Highlands then was; not the strictly even threaded and multi-coloured cloth we have today. The word for the basic woollen material in Gaelic is *breacan*, meaning a large chequered blanket. In time 'tartan' became the recognised word for the Highlanders' dress, and two weights came into being - a lighter one for the womenfolk, and a heavier and coarser one for men at work or at war. At the end of the 16th century standardisation of the pattern of the tartan had not yet arrived, and Highlanders used their clothing as camouflage when hunting, stealing cattle or in armed conflict with other clans; accepting what was produced by the weavers in different areas, who used what dyes they could prepare from local lichens and plants, steeped in various peculiar and particular liquids. The resultant material was usually speckled in a chequered or mottled or herringbone weave.

By the year 1600 Scottish soldiers could be recognised by their mottled and fringed cloaks, with their belts worn over their cloaks. The cloak-like garment was the origin of the *plaide* (Gaelic), meaning simply a blanket, and was know in time as the *faileadh-mor* (Gaelic) or big kilt, which in due course became the *faileadh-beag* (Gaelic) or little kilt, the later becoming shortened to the philabeg or filibeg. To make a plaid the Highland weaver put on his loom enough threads on the warp for the least five plaiden ells or about 16 feet. The width of the plaid was usually about 4 feet. This figure of approximately 54 inches was beyond the reach of a handloom shuttle, so two widths of between 20 and 26 inches depending on the pattern by about 16 feet long were woven, matched up for pattern side by side, and then sewn together down the middle. Later, once the machine age had arrived, plaids of 54 inches wide could be woven with no middle join. It might be of interest to learn that a standard Scottish ell measured 37.06 inches, and the plaiden ell equalled 38.42 inches. When the philabeg became popular one width of the handloom material of between the 20 and 26 inches was ample to make a suitable pleated garment for any height of Highlander. Gradually, however, over the years the kilt has lengthened. The modern machine width of a standard tartan is, as has been said, 54 inches, which is termed 'double-width'. If a special order for a kilt is placed for a not too well known tartan, then the machine width may well be 27 inches, or 'single-width'.

Prior to the arrival of Bonnie Prince Charlie, the Young Pretender, in the Western Highlands in August 1745, there was no completely rigid observation of Clan or family tartans, though this was beginning to come about. Highland soldiers serving the Crown wore standard dress and equipment, but all persons living above the Highland Line, which was and is from the southern end of Loch Lomond north east to Aberdeen, wore what their local weavers found most easy to supply, from the dyed wools which came to hand. There is a well known painting of about 1660 showing a Highland Chieftain, which could possibly have been Lord Breadalbane, and throught it is a very decorative outfit that he is wearing, there is no regular sett or repeat in the material. There is also a painting, among others, of two your MacDonald boys, painted just after the Disarming Act of 1746 became law, which shows them wearing what can only be described as three different tartans.

So now we arrive at the year 1746.

Culloden and the Proscription

On the 16th April 1746, Prince Charles Edward Stuart's exhausted and ill-equipped Highland army was routed at Culloden, near Inverness, by William, the Duke of Cumberland's regular troops in under half an hour. The Jacobite uprising had caused considerable alarm in the Government in London. There had been previous attempts to curb the Highlanders in their warlike activities, and there were Disarming Acts passed in 1716 and 1725. Within only months of the battle, if it can be called that, of Culloden another Disarming Act had been passed on 12th August 1746. This Act, which discouraged the use of the Gealic language, proscribed the wearing of Highland dress and its material accoutrements, and the use of any tartan by men and boys; but it did not apply to Highland Regiments, women or landowners or their sons. The penalty for breaking the new law was six months imprisonment on the first offence, and a maximum of seven years transportation for the second offence. This proscription was a terrible burden on the Highlanders and their families. For example, from where did they quickly get their new clothes, even if they could afford them? If they did not procure them they were in real trouble, for troops in the early years of the Act covered the Highlands, and when the Act was first passed had orders to shoot on sight any person "dressed in the Highland garb". In consequence the art and the knowledge of the waving of Clan, District and family tartans, such as they were, was gradually lost, as the older weavers (men) and the producers of the dyed wools (women) died off.

Effect of the repeal

The un-tartaned Highlands remained peaceful for the next few years, but help for the national dress was on the way. In 1788 the Highland Society was formed in London, and they strenuously campaigned for the repeal of the Disarming Act. With the assistance of John Graham, the Marquis of Graham, who later became the Duke of Montrose, a bill was introduced in Parliament in London, and the Act was repealed, without opposition, on 17th June 1782, after over 35 years on the Statute Books. It is interesting to note that between 1740 and 1815 there were 86 Highland Regiments formed for military service. Also, that after the defeat at Culloden a cycle of depopulation of the Highlands had begun with many men and families emigrating overseas with sheep taking their place on the hills and in the glens. It followed that the development of the Highland dress and the tartan had been broken, but gradually after 1782 the weaving of tartan was begun again.

By 1800 William Wilson and Son, who had their factory at

Bannockburn, were manufacturing a few tartans, other then military ones, and by 1822 were producing 150, when King George IV visited Edinburgh. There are probably one thousand tartans today. In about 1815 the Highland Society of London came on the scene again. It is assumed that the Members of that Society decided to record all Clan tartans.

Accordingly they approached all Clan Chiefs, and asked them for a sample of their authenticated tartan. Many of them sent such a sample, but some did not, or were unable to, having no Chief. All the same by about 1816 the Society managed to produce a list of tartans showing the setts, accurate as far as possible, and this included the Clan MacArthur, but not the single stripe tartan worn by Clansmen and Clanswomen today.

The method of weaving tartan

Let us now look at how a piece of tartan is woven. A given number of threads of each colour are stretched length-wise on the loom. As an example I shall use the present day Clan MacArthur tartan. Accordingly we have 64 black theads, 12 green, 24 black, 60 green and 6 yellow. A weaver would understand that, but it only takes us halfway across the sett, and to complete the pattern it goes on, that is back in reverse to the beginning, with 60 green, 24 black, 2 green and 64 black, then you start again with 12 green, etc. That makes the warp, and the exact same thread counts will produce the crosswise weft, which when complete from black 64 to yellow 6 and back to green 12, in both directions, will result in the present day Clan MacArthur sett of a perfect square. It will be seen that only three colours of thread are used, but it must be noted that the old vegetable hand-dyed wools produced a lighter coloured tartan than today's chemical dyes do; though a lighter chemically coloured tartan, called 'ancient', is available nowadays. But what about the 1816 London recorded Clan MacArthur tartan? It again was only of three coloured threads, the same black, green and yellow, but in different thread counts. These were black 30, green 4, black 8, green 36, yellow 4, green 36, yellow 4, green 36, black 8, green 4, arriving back at black 30. These thread numbers of course produce two yellow stripes crossing the sett in both directions, creating a pleasing effect. How has this, presumably older sett, been lost?

Prince Charlie's "Grandsons" and the Tartan Boom

We must go back to history, and to Bonnie Prince Charlie, who was born in Rome in 1720, and died there in 1788, having married Princess Louse of Stolberg at the age of 52, in the hope of producing a male heir. He apparently did not. The mother of Charles Edward Stuart belonged to the Sobieska Royal House of Poland. Round about the year 1817 two young brothers named John and Charles Allen arrived in London, and then moved to Edinburgh, claiming to be the legitimate grandsons of Prince Charles Edward. They were right royally received everywhere they went, and Lord Lovat settled them in due time in a house on the island in the River Beauly, not far from Inverness. Prior to that they had lived off and on for nearly four years on Lochawe-side.

The brothers produced a tattered manuscript of 38 pages dated 1721 of 75 'authentic' tartans. Then in June 1829 more pages were added showing more Clans and families. The two Allens by now called themselves John Sobieski and Charles Edward Stuart. Sir Walter Scott, assisted by General David Stewart of Garth, had arranged the visit of King George IV to Edinburgh in August 1822, and this Royal appearance in Scotland had caused a tremendous upsurge in the use of tartan. Wilsons at Bannockburn had to install an extra 40 looms. By the way, Wilsons were in business from 1720 to 1976, when they closed down, having been the most successful tartan manufacturers in their time. Needless to say the two brothers John Sobieski and Charles Edward Stuart took full advantage of this colossal demand for tartan.

'Vestiarium Scoticum'

In 1842 William Tait, a publisher in Edinburgh, produced a limited edition of 50 copies of a book called *Vestiarium Scoticum*. It was sold at 10 guineas a copy, a fair price in those days. The Introduction and Notes were written by John Sobieski Stuart, with the illustrations of 75 tartans by Charles Edward Stuart. It was a large book, and the tartans were shown in full colour; but nearly all of them were unknown to tartan manufacturers of that time. However, these particular tartans soon became popular, to the extent that they were quickly widely known, and are seemingly recognised today. I have it on good authority that the Clan MacArthur tartan with the single yellow thread count of 6, appeared in the *Vestiarium Scoticum*, and presumably because everything the two brothers said or printed was taken as gospel, because people wanted to believe, it was accepted by the manufacturers.

So a MacArthur from the 1850s onwards, ordering a kilt or other Highland dress for himself or his wife and family, would have been shown only one tartan by his tailor, such as J. Spittal and Son in Edinburgh, as the tailor in turn would only have been shown one tartan by the weaving factory. Thus the double lined tartan, which in 1816 was shown as the original and authentic Clan MacArthur Tartan, was 'lost'. However, I have in my possession a piece of that double yellow striped tartan, and I have had it photocopied in colour, a copy of which I have sent to the editor of the "Round Table". I am sure he will find it of interest.

In 1845 the firm of J. Menzies of Edinburgh published from the Allen (Stuart) brothers another book called *The Costume of the Clans*, and it seems that they for some considerable time continued to delve deeply into the Highland way of life, both social and domestic, as well as into the local costumes. John died in 1872 aged about 76; Charles died in 1880 aged about 83, having in their later years gone to live on the continent. They were both buried at Eskdale Church not far from Beauly. Much more could be written about those two, but I feel that I have given you enough to fill out a picture of them.

Hand-woven MacArthur kilt over £200 (or $500) in 1990

If any Clan society Member was interested in having an eight-yard kilt length hand woven in Scotland, of either of the tartans, if he could find such a weaver, as there are very, very few left, he should expect to pay at least £25 a yard. That is, a hand woven Clan MacArthur kilt, which of course is the best, and would last for years and years, would now cost over £200 initially, with the making up charge on top. A machine produced kilt length would be somewhat cheaper, but not all that much, for a certain amount of the cost goes on setting up the machine, especially for a short length.

A second Tartan Boom

And now lastly. There is a Scottish Tartans Society at Comrie in Perthshire, which maintains a Register of All Publicly Known Tartans, and its archives are extensive, together with its museum. It was inaugurated by the Lord Lyon King of Arms, Sir Thomas Innes of Learney, on 13th May 1963, and I am given to understand that the Lyon Court keeps a watching brief on what goes on in the Society. I have mentioned the sudden surge in demand for the tartan, which took place from 1822 onwards, but it seems that the same thing is occurring again today. The couturier houses in London, Paris and New York are using tartans extensively in creating their exclusive day and evening dress designs for women, not forgetting the outfits for men, who also want to be in the tartan fashion.

Map of Part of Argyll

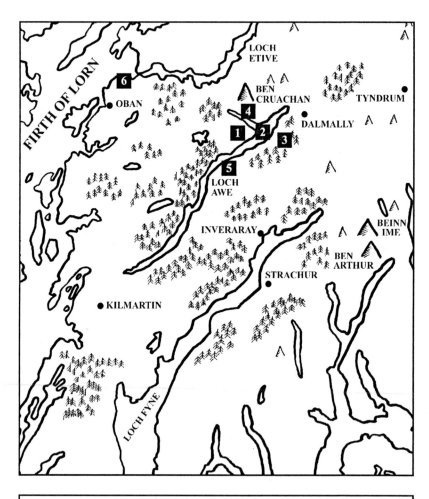

1. Tirivadich	4. Pass of Brander
2. Inishail	5. Innischonnel Castle
3. Inistrynich	6. Dunnstaffnage Castle

The Pass of Brander

My father took me one year by road from Dunoon to the Argyllshire Gathering (Highland Games) held annually at Oban. That was well before the Cruachan hydroelectric power station was built in 1964. As we drove along the side of Loch Awe, approaching the Pass of Brander, I was told about the battle that took place there in August 1308 between the army of Robert the Bruce and the MacDougalls. Coming out of the gorge I was shown where the actual battle occurred, and where the heavily defeated MacDougall clansmen were immediately buried, because there were so many of them slain. If anyone wishes to see the site it is still there to this day, almost 700 years on.

Leaving the gorge and passing the small modern dam holding back the waters of the loch from the River Awe, look to your left as you start down a slope to a petrol station on the left 200 yards further on, before the bridge over the river. If you can, stop and get out, for you are now on the battleground, and some people say they can feel something strange about the area where so many men died. Now look again left, down the sloping field to the River Awe, and across it to the area beyond. There you will see many loose stone mounds, which mark the MacDougall graves. But... how did this all happen?

Robert the Bruce (Robert I of Scotland) was crowned as King at Scone in March 1306. He then set about trying to build the country into a governable whole, and this meant controlling many of the leading Clans. In the summer of 1308 it became the turn of the MacDougalls of Lorne to be dealt with, and so Bruce, gathering together an army, marched on their Clan lands to the west of Loch Awe. He wished to capture their strong point, Dunstaffnage Castle, on the cost a few miles north of Oban, commanding the sea entrance to Loch Etive, but the only short way to make the approach was through the Pass of Brander. The weather was good in the middle of that August, so Bruce was able to advance quickly. The MacDougalls however, were ready for him and had blocked the narrow road with a small fort in the Pass of Brander with steep hillside to their left and the loch to their right.

Bruce was not going to make progress easily. But he was not a commander of men for nothing. He halted his column, which was obvious to the scouts of the fort. Then, under cover of darkness, he sent a strong but mobile party of men up the hillside and forward to await developments. At first light, when the MacDougall scouts could view Bruce's halted force strung out along the roadway, they were astonished to see the rear start to march eastwards, shortly followed by the centre.

They assumed that Bruce was in retreat, and reported to the fort accordingly, who stood down.

At the noise of the battle, the party which had been sent higher up the hill by Bruce in the night and which had remained hidden in the morning mist on the hilltop, now fulfilled their roll. They charged into the flank of the MacDougalls and the combined pressure drove those Clansmen down the slope into the River Awe, where many died. The way was now open to advance on the Castle of Dunstaffnage, about 15 miles further west.

Dunstaffnage Castle Falls

Leaving the battlefield at the Pass of Brander, Bruce and his army marched to Dunstaffnage Castle and camped close by in the area south of the Castle. Three days later, despite being well provisioned, the elderly Alexander MacDougall of Lorne decided to surrender the Castle. But Bruce did not tarry there, for he had other urgent matters to attend to, and so returned east, his initial mission having been accomplished. He left his personal representative in charge of the Castle, with the title of Constable, and the King's appointment was Sir Arthur Campbell. How long Sir Arthur actually remained in that post cannot readily be ascertained. However, over a period of 160 years there were Constables consecutively appointed by the Crown to hold the post, including the employment of a MacDougall, and a member of the Stewart family of Innermeath. (Researchers will not readily find the location of Innermeath because the name has been changed over the years. These Stewarts of Innermeath held property that was just south of Forteviot in Perthshire, with the River Meath running through the area. But some time in most recent, but still ancient, years the name was changed to Invermay, with the river then called May.) [Research can sometimes be a bit trying!]

With such knowledge as I had and research gleaned I cannot find that any MacArthurs ever held any post connected with the Castle of Dunstaffnage between the dates of 1308 and 1470. In that year King James III of Scotland decided that he would hand over for all time the responsibility of looking after the Castle of Dunstaffnage to Colin Campbell, 1st Earl of Argyll. The latter, in turn, appointed a younger son to be the permanent holder of the Captaincy of Dunstaffnage, along with the ground adjacent. It has remained in that family ever since, and today there is a Campbell as 22nd Hereditary Captain of Dunstaffnage. If anyone can find out or happens to possess more detail as to what happened between 1308 and 1470 I am sure that the Editor would be very pleased to receive it, so that all of us might learn more of the past.

Innischonnel Castle

The MacArthurs could well have been involved in the battle of the Pass of Brander in 1308, for they were rewarded with land in due course. They did, however, hold the Captaincy of a castle later on. There was a Charles MacArthur who was a witness to various major charters locally and in Stirling, Glasgow, and Edinburgh for the 2nd Earl of Argyll, before the latter was killed at Flodden in 1513. Duncan MacArthur succeeded his father, Charles, in about 1525, and in due time became the attorney for the 4th Earl of Argyll, holding an even more enhanced position than his father, so much so that he was appointed as Captain of the Earl's castle of Innischonnel on an island on Loch Awe, along with his other duties. The Earl's ancestors had left Innischonnel Castle by about 1450, when the new castle was built at Inveraray. The Loch Awe castle then became a prison for the use of the Earl, being only approachable by rowing boat, as it is to this day.

But Duncan was not all that popular with the Campbells of

Inverawe, who felt that he had taken over many of their duties, and so a happening occurred. Duncan, one day in 1567, was fishing on Loch Awe with some family and friends. They were approached by boat by the Inverawe Campbells and, in the ensuing fight on the water, Duncan, with others of the fishing party, was drowned. The Earl, on hearing of the incident, was not best pleased and ordered reparations to be made, appointing Patrick, a son of Duncan, to be the Captain of Innischonnel Castle. While he was in charge in 1578 he held some important prisoners for the Earl. They were John MacDonald, son and heir to the MacDonald of Castle Camus on Skye, Laughlin MacLean, young chief of Duart on Mull, and John MacLean, his uncle.

Patrick was succeeded in 1579 by his son, Duncan, as the Captain of Innischonnel Castle, but unfortunately, he was not a success, being forfeited for theft in 1613. Nothing further is heard from him, but then having been declared forfeit he would have left the area with his family, if he had any. The Earl appointing a MacLachlan to fill the vacant captaincy at the castle.

The Great Highland Bagpipe

The pipe that might be said to be the very early forerunner of the Scottish Great Highland Bagpipe could have been in existence before the Pharaohs were building their pyramids in Egypt. It consisted of a reed made of two pieces of thin wood bound together, which vibrated to provide a noise when submitted to air pressure being partially within the player's mouth. This reed was inserted into a hollow wooden or bone tube, with probably only six or seven holes (the eight-hole modern chanter came later), which ended with a suitably shaped hollow piece of sheep or goat's horn to amplify the sound.

This rough handmade musical instrument would usually have been found in the possession of a youthful and lonely shepherd boy, played to break the monotony of his working day. It could have originated in several places in the Near East, but just possibly it came into being in what is now called the Punjab in India or in Pakistan, moving on to what we know as Afghanistan, to Persia (Iran), through Asia Minor to Egypt, and so to the Holy Land, Greece and the Roman Empire in the 1st and 2nd centuries, of course becoming refined on the way. Early, it was known as a 'shawm', but later as an 'aulos' by the Greeks.

In due course it arrived in Brittany, but had by then developed a blow pipe, a bag as a reservoir for air, and a single-reeded drone with a better-made reed in the chanter, perhaps now with eight holes, one being at the rear, producing nine notes. Travel progress continued, to England and Ireland, and pipes were found in Scotland at the time of the Picts in the 8th and 9th centuries, but not yet quite like the musical instrument we know today.

It would require some little space to go into the slow but steady development of the modern two tenor and one bass drones of the Great Highland Bagpipe, but suffice it to say it has become an instrument that can be played by the amateur or professional, and listened to by young and old with enjoyment, and often with considerable knowledge of the tunes played. But Scotland itself has not been the only country to benefit from a stirring and the making of a foot-tapping sound, for our pipes are now to be found all over the world, in bands both civil and military. In the USA, Canada, Australia, New Zealand, the Middle East, Pakistan and India, to name but a few. Gurkas from Nepal have been found to be natural players, and once trained by the Army School of Piping in Edinburgh can produce a first-class sound, and compete with the best. Of course, the individual player has also carried his skill worldwide, both for his own pleasure as well as for that of others.

Famous piping families

Let us now have a quick look at some famous piping families of about the 18th century and earlier. There were the Cummings in Badenoch and Strathspey, the MacGregors in Glenlyon, the MacKays in Gairloch and on Raasay, the Macintyres in Rannoch, as well as the MacArthurs at Peingown, near Duntulm, and the MacCrimmons at Boreraig, near Dunvegan, both on Skye, the last two having their own piping schools. Over the years all these pipers improved the music of the bagpipe, until its steady advancement was suddenly halted by the embargo placed on all playing of the pipes by an Act of Parliament in London. This took place in the autumn of 1746, after the battle at Culloden in April that year. The Act was repealed in 1782, and in the Highlands the kilt and the pipes happily came into use once again, but as far as the latter were concerned part of the skill of the playing and the knowledge of the national instrument had been lost. Fortuitously, they have now more than fully recovered; with pipe music being written once again, often in a somewhat more modern fashion.

An unforgiving instrument

The bagpipe, tuned by the player so that all four reeds sound in harmony, is a versatile but perhaps an unforgiving musical instrument; being affected, among other things, by heat and cold (as are the

29

piper's fingers!). The same tune being played individually by a number of pipers in a competition can quite easily produce slightly different interpretations. Hence the problem faced by piping judges at Highland Games. In a Band competition, however, all the pipes are tuned to one set of pipes, so that the whole band sounds as one. Then presentation and accuracy, as well as marching, turnout, and deportment come into their own. The Great Highland Bagpipe is a wonderful instrument, and has raised the blood of Scots on many occasions, not the least of which have been in battle, modern as well as ancient. Separately, the playing of the classical pipe music, the *Piobaireachd*, is an exact art unto itself; and has to be listened to carefully to be fully understood.

If anyone should wish further information it is suggested that a copy of *The Book of the Bagpipe* be obtained. It is a small inexpensive book written in 1999 by Hugh Cheape, and is well worth having. It is published by The Appletree Press, Ltd., in Belfast, and includes two pages of details for further reading.

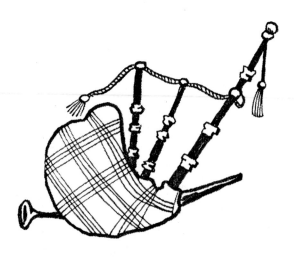

Highland Games
& Highland Dancing

I have gleaned that in the years long gone, when the warmer spring and summer weather had arrived in the Highlands of Scotland, and the young women and children had taken themselves off to the shielings in the hills for the sake of better pasturage for the cattle, the young men in the villages often found themselves with little to do. To fill in the time when the house repairs and other farm and domestic ploys had been completed on a daily basis, athletic sports were held in a purely friendly manner. Apart from running hill races there were jumping over a height, putting a stone, or throwing one over a high bar. But perhaps the greater skill and strength was reserved for the tossing of a tree trunk, so that it fell exactly at 12 o'clock away from the thrower. As time went on these simple pastimes became competitive between adjacent friendly villages, and so Highland Games could have been said to have been born. They were not, however, fully recognized as such till about 1820.

The fiddle and the bagpipes were, of course, part of everyday village and Clan life, and dancing took place informally, but especially on festive days and at weddings. These dances were made up of a number of couples dancing together in sets of six or more persons, but there were individual dances as well. The oldest is The Highland Fling, based on the red deer stag on the hills, because the hands of the dancer are held in the shape of antlers. It is danced on the spot, and this could originally have been indicative of the stag stamping its front hooves in the rutting season. The Sword Dance is a show of triumph after a successful incident or battle, when the victor laid his own sword on top of that of his defeated opponent in the form of a cross, and danced over them. The *Seann Triubhas* came much later, after the battle of Culloden in April 1746, when the wearing of the kilt was banned by the Parliament in London. It signifies that the dancer is wishing to get rid of unwanted trousers, forced on him by an edict outwith his own land.

There are other dances that nowadays appear in Highland Games programmes; namely, The Strathspey, The Reel, and The Reel of Tulloch, but they are all based on Scottish Country Dances, though Highland in nature, but now choreographed for competition purposes.

It will be realised that all contests between athletes at the early all-male games were of a light-hearted nature; but now, on the dancing platform, it seems that the winning of a prize among the male and greater number of female dancers—and particularly among the mothers—is a must!

The Laird of Milton's Daughter

A Scottish Jig

Scottish country dance history began in 1651 when John Playford published his first book of country dances. Before that there were no written descriptions of dances even through many of them were named. One may wonder at the title 'country dancing' when most dances look so much like ballroom dancing, but they belong to every class of society and to every part of the country. Originally, this type of dancing belonged to the court, but through the democratic nature of Scottish society they were danced in the barn as well as the castle.

Scottish country dancing is not folk or peasant dancing: it is the ballroom dancing of Scotland. The elegance and dignity natural to the ballroom is shown in the movements and manners. The actual steps had their origin in French ballet, while the manners – the use of hands and social spirit – came from the French court during the period known as the Auld Alliance.

Such dances were composed over the years for various reasons: to honour a person, a place, or a happening. They have been danced by the highest and the lowest in the land, from ballroom to byre, as a social event, or simply to keep warm. Usually the name of a dance gives a good indication of why it was written, but sometimes this is not so. For example 'The Duran Ranger' comes from a salmon fly. 'Hamilton House' was created because the son of a Border laird eloped with the younger sister of his bride-to-be the night before the wedding. 'The Reel of the Fifty-first Division' came into being in 1940 because Highland officers in a prison-of-war camp were allowed nothing Scottish. They produced a St. Andrew's Cross every time they danced the reel!

Dances continue to be produced and, if found suitable, are published by the Royal Scottish Country Dance Society. Such a dance is 'The Laird of Milton's Daughter'.

Background of 'Milton's Daughter'

In 1950 I was working for the Scottish mercantile firm of Mackinnon, Mackenzie and Co. in Calcutta, India. Patricia, my wife, entered the Elgin Nursing Home there in early October and on the 10th of that month, Mary Emelia MacArthur-Moir was born.

In my free time from office work I taught Scottish country dancing at the Scots kirk hall attached to the church in Dalhousie Square, near the Black Hole of Calcutta (1756). Among the dancers was a good friend of mine, Donald Shaw, Lord Craigmyle, who worked in the same office, being a cousin of Kenneth Mackay, the Earl of Inchcape, who had considerable shipping interests in the East, including the firm for which we worked.

Lord Craigmyle decided to mark Mary's birth and, early in 1951, he devised and presented here with here own Scottish country dance, a jig, called 'The Laird of Milton's Daughter', her father being the Laird of Milton at Dunoon in Argyllshire.

Later that year Pat, Mary and I went on home leave and, in Dunoon, we danced with Cowal Country Dance Club. There we tried out Mary's dance, and they liked it. So I asked Mr W G M Christian, the organist of the church in Kirn, to write a tune. This he kindly agreed to do and wrote several before he was satisfied and he gave me the final one. Shortly after that the family and I went back to India, and the dance continued to be danced in Cowal – now to its own tune.

By the time I came to live in Edinburgh in 1956, on leaving India, the dance was fairly well known in the west of Scotland, but not in the east. However, in about 1958 I met Miss M F Hadden, the secretary of the Royal Scottish Country Dance Society, and she asked me for a copy of the dance and music. I gave them to her and forgot about it.

WORDS FROM THE CHIEF

Five years later, in April 1963, I received a letter from Miss Hadden telling me that the Society was collecting new, as well as old, dances, and they were publishing Mary's dance in the yearly book. She asked if I could please arrange, therefore, for Lord Craigmyle and Mr Christian to assign the copyright to the Society. This was done, and the dance published as No 10 in a book of *Twelve Modern Scottish Country Dances in Traditional Form*.

Over 100 dances had been examined before the 12 were selected to make up Book 22.

The jig is now danced throughout Scotland, and a Lismor tape by Ian Holmes and his Scottish Dance Band has been produced in Glasgow which includes the tune. Other dance tunes on the tape are the Eightsome Reel, a set of Strathspeys and Jigs and 'The Duke and Duchess of Edinburgh', composed in honour of the wedding of HRH The Princess Elizabeth to HRH The Prince Phillip, Duke of Edinburgh.

For those interested, the Book 22 referred to above was made copyright in 1963 in the United States by the Royal Scottish Dance society. The tape (number LICS 5097) referred to is by:

Lismore Recordings, Peter Hamilton (Music),
42 Kilmarnock Road, Glasgow, Scotland, G41 3NH

The Stone of Scone
Originally known as
The Stone of Destiny

When at school, many years ago, our history teacher aroused the interest of his class in the early Scottish period, with particular reference to Wallace and Bruce from 1270 to 1329. That is to say, from the birth of Sir William (1270-1305) to the death of King Robert I of Scotland (1306-1329). There would appear to be several misleading statements in the article referred to above, but I would wish to leave these for other interested persons to comment upon, while I concentrate on The Stone of Destiny, as it was originally known, but sometimes referred to as Jacob's Pillow. As far as I am aware it only became known as the Stone of Scone when King Edward I of England (1272-1307) had it removed from Scone in Perthshire to London in the year 1296.

The rolling Stone

The Stone which we know today is a block of sandstone measuring 26 inches long, 16 inches wide and 11 inches in depth with a weight of 336 pounds, having two iron rings, one at each end, for carrying purposes. But where can one see today this ancient Stone, the visual trappings of Scottish sovereignty? Not at Dunstaffnage Castle in Argyll nor In King Edward's Coronation Chair in Westminster Abbey in London. Why? Because it is right here in Edinburgh Castle, along with the Honours of Scotland: the Crown, the Sceptre, and the Sword of State. All four of these important items in Scottish history are housed in a special display at the summit of the Castle, adjacent to the Scottish National War Memorial. Let us now have a look at how such an historic and valuable object as the Stone arrived at its present, hopefully peaceful and final, resting place; for if all be true about it, and not just hearsay, it has been on the move from Israel and within Scotland and England for well over 2,000 years.

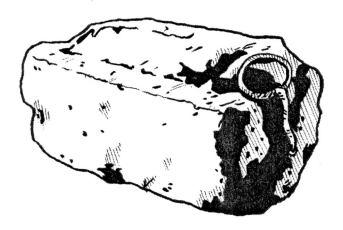

Holy relic

The Stone of Destiny has for a very long time in Scotland been considered to be a Holy Relic. It was said to have been a pillow for Jacob in early biblical times, and is, therefore, known to a few persons in Scotland to this day as Jacob's Pillow. It was thought to have been brought to Scotland through Egypt, Sicily, Spain and Ireland. Whether any or all of the foregoing is true or not, it certainly did arrive in ancient times in what is now mid-Argyll. There it was used in the crowning ceremonies of Dalriadic Kings of Iona, Dunadd and Dunstaffnage, when the Kingdom of Dalriada existed from roughly 400 to 800 AD. In about 850 AD Kenneth MacAlpine, who reigned from not earlier than 843 to 858 as the first King of the Picts and the Scots, decided to leave the west coast because of the constant raids made by Vikings along the whole of that area bordered by the sea. He moved his capital to Scone in mid-Scotland, a much safer place, and took The Stone of Destiny with him. The Priory of Scone was founded in 1120 with Augustinian monks, and in 1164 it became an Abbey, and so the Stone was placed in the safe keeping of the Abbot. So it remained, close to and for use on the Moot Hill, a small artificial mound there to this day, on which subsequent royal enthronements took place. The Abbey no longer exists.

Edward moves the Stone

That peaceful situation changed in Scone in 1296. Edward I of England had subjugated Scotland, and had organized several places across southern Scotland, from Berwick to Aryshire, where the nobility, land owners and other important Scots could show homage and give their signed allegiance to the English King. These lists of names became known as the Ragman Rolls. But Edward was not entirely satisfied, and so he decided to remove the Stone (of Destiny) to England, as it was to him the outward symbol of Scottish sovereignty. To have the Stone in his hands would mean, he presumably felt, that he had complete control over Scotland. At the same time as the homage was being paid the Abbot of Scone Abbey was notified that a strong military party would shortly arrive to collect the Stone, and escort it to Westminster Abbey in London. So after a few days when the slow-moving military escort, with most likely its oxen-drawn four-wheeled wooden waggon, had arrived, the Stone was quietly handed over, for its 450-mile ignominious journey to London.

A question remains

But was it the real Stone of Destiny (Jacob's Pillow)? The soldiers would not know what they were supposed to carry south, as none would have seen it before. It is considered by a few that the Stone of Destiny was of black basalt, with two lifting rings, but somewhat larger than the present Stone of Scone. In between the time of the notification and the collection the Abbot could have ordered a substitute stone, but it would have had to be of sandstone locally quarried. Who would have been wiser, except the monks? Could it be significant that there was, as far as I am aware, no hindrance from the Scots as the Stone traveled slowly from Scone to the Scottish border at Berwick? Were some other people also privy to a secret, if there actually was one?

Plans gang agley

While all this was going on in Scotland King Edward in London had ordered a special wooden Coronation Chair (some call it a Throne) to be made, with a suitable opening under the seat to receive the Stone from Scone, so that as each future monarch was crowned in Westminster Abbey he sat on the sovereignty of Scotland. The Stone (of Scone) duly arrived, after a long and tedious journey, and was greeted with much excitement, but when it was presented to its future home consternation reigned. It would not go into the recess. The measurement details, seemingly sent forward from Scotland, had been correctly taken except for one very important one. The overall measurement of the two pieces of metal let into the two ends of the Stone and holding the lifting rings was not accurate. What to do? Well it was decided, apparently, to file down one of the metal ring retainers which stuck out, but not so much as would weaken it and so the lifting ring. This done, the Stone was at last introduced to its new home for the next 700 years, except for a short period of four months beginning on 25th December 1950, of which more anon. By the Treaty of Northampton between England and Scotland, ratified in 1328, the Stone of Scone was to be returned to Scotland, but it never was.

Spirited away and returned

The Stone remained quietly (but see below) in its Coronation Chair in the Abbey, which was used each time a monarch came to be crowned, including Queen Elizabeth II (Queen Elizabeth I in Scotland) in 1953. That peaceful situation very rapidly changed early in the morning of Christmas Day 1950. Four young Scots managed with some difficulty to get the Stone out of the Chair, and out of the Abbey, and it was spirited away over the border, not to be seen again for four long months much to the worry of the authorities concerned. It was then voluntarily returned to official custodianship, by being left near the altar of the ruined Abbey of Arbroath. It will be recalled that it was at the Abbey of Arbroath the Declaration of Arbroath (also known as the Declaration of Independence) was drafted and sealed in April 1320, by the gathering of some 39 Scottish nobles. The Declaration was then sent to Pope John XXII to confirm their determination to maintain the independence of Scotland, and the support of King Robert! Presumably, because of its historic connections, this particular site was chosen on which to return the Stone of Scone.

An agreement honoured

The return of the Stone to London in 1951 was seemingly muted, but it was to be used once again in its official capacity, for the Coronation of our present Queen, as mentioned above. Subsequently, after official negotiations had taken place, and perhaps because Scotland was shortly to have its own Parliament, it was decided to send the Stone of Scone home. Accordingly, on 30th November 1996 the Stone was piped over the border at the bridge over the river Tweed at Berwick in a motor cavalcade: compare a wooden waggon. It was then taken to the Palace of Holyrood House. A few days later the Stone was transported, with due ceremony, up the Royal Mile between welcoming crowds, to Edinburgh Castle, where, as I have said, it can be seen by all today.

Myth? Fable? Truth?

This last paragraph of this lengthy article/story has now been reached. It has been an extremely interesting exercise writing it, from schoolboy learning days up to now; research having been necessary from the former onwards. I would not, however, wish any reader to take what I have written as gospel, as I am not a trained historian, though I have always much enjoyed the reading of Scottish history as a subject. I am romantically still inclined to think that the Stone now in Edinburgh Castle was possibly a substitute hurriedly arranged by a patriotic Abbot; and I hope that the Stone of Destiny, brought over all those years ago from Ireland to modern Argyll, may one day be found, most likely quite by accident, in the Scone area. I leave each one of you to form your own opinion, guided no doubt by what has been written by eminent historians over the years.

MacArthur Society in Britain

A Branch of Clan Arthur

The MacArthur Society was founded in 1974 and Clan Arthur was reformed in 2003 with the inauguration of our first Chief for over 230 years.

Clan Arthur welcomes new members from people with the name (or related to the name) of Arthur, Arthurson, Carter, Dewar, MacArtair, MacArthur, MacArtor, MacCarter, MacIndeor and all spelling variations.

For UK membership contact:

Robert D MacArthur, FSA Scot
3 Highfield Road
Scone
Perth
PH2 6RE
Scotland

For international membership please visit **www.clanarthur.co.uk**

www.clannarthur.com

Oor Arthur: An exploration of Scottish Arthurian tradition and theory.

Sons of Arthur: Clan Arthur's history, traditions, culture and people.

House of Arthur: Online Scottish Clan store - Tartan, jewellery, Highland Dress, books, maps and gifts.

Arthurian Trail: Interactive map of Arthurian sites in Scotland.

Clann News: All the latest Arthurian and Clan gossip from the media.

Clann Forum: Visitor book and online chat room.

Clann Home Fund: Clann Arthur Visitor Centre fund appeal.

Links: Links to Clan, genealogical and historical web sites.

The Future: Information on MacArthur Societies across the globe and the international newsletter *The Wee Round Table*.

Forthcoming Booklets

The Arthurian Lake
A study of the Arthurian landscape and Brythonic tradition surrounding Loch Lomond. *Available 2006.*

Arthur's Battles
An exploration of King Arthur's battles in the Scottish landscape. *Available 2006.*

MacArthur
A complete guide to the history, tradition and culture of Clan Arthur. *Available 2006.*